Fun Facts & Trivia
1972 - A Year In Review

ISBN: 9798787704839

INDEX

FIRST EDITION

1972

January
M	T	W	T	F	S	S
					1	2
3	4	5	6	7	8	9
10	11	12	13	14	15	16
17	18	19	20	21	22	23
24	25	26	27	28	29	30
31						

☽:8 ●:16 ☾:23 ○:30

February
M	T	W	T	F	S	S
	1	2	3	4	5	6
7	8	9	10	11	12	13
14	15	16	17	18	19	20
21	22	23	24	25	26	27
28	29					

☽:7 ●:15 ☾:21 ○:29

March
M	T	W	T	F	S	S
		1	2	3	4	5
6	7	8	9	10	11	12
13	14	15	16	17	18	19
20	21	22	23	24	25	26
27	28	29	30	31		

☽:8 ●:15 ☾:22 ○:29

April
M	T	W	T	F	S	S
					1	2
3	4	5	6	7	8	9
10	11	12	13	14	15	16
17	18	19	20	21	22	23
24	25	26	27	28	29	30

☽:7 ●:13 ☾:20 ○:28

May
M	T	W	T	F	S	S
1	2	3	4	5	6	7
8	9	10	11	12	13	14
15	16	17	18	19	20	21
22	23	24	25	26	27	28
29	30	31				

☽:6 ●:13 ☾:20 ○:28

June
M	T	W	T	F	S	S
			1	2	3	4
5	6	7	8	9	10	11
12	13	14	15	16	17	18
19	20	21	22	23	24	25
26	27	28	29	30		

☽:4 ●:11 ☾:18 ○:26

July
M	T	W	T	F	S	S
					1	2
3	4	5	6	7	8	9
10	11	12	13	14	15	16
17	18	19	20	21	22	23
24	25	26	27	28	29	30
31						

☽:4 ●:10 ☾:18 ○:26

August
M	T	W	T	F	S	S
	1	2	3	4	5	6
7	8	9	10	11	12	13
14	15	16	17	18	19	20
21	22	23	24	25	26	27
28	29	30	31			

☽:2 ●:9 ☾:17 ○:24 ☽:31

September
M	T	W	T	F	S	S
				1	2	3
4	5	6	7	8	9	10
11	12	13	14	15	16	17
18	19	20	21	22	23	24
25	26	27	28	29	30	

●:7 ☾:15 ○:23 ☽:29

October
M	T	W	T	F	S	S
						1
2	3	4	5	6	7	8
9	10	11	12	13	14	15
16	17	18	19	20	21	22
23	24	25	26	27	28	29
30	31					

●:7 ☾:15 ○:22 ☽:29

November
M	T	W	T	F	S	S
		1	2	3	4	5
6	7	8	9	10	11	12
13	14	15	16	17	18	19
20	21	22	23	24	25	26
27	28	29	30			

●:6 ☾:14 ○:20 ☽:27

December
M	T	W	T	F	S	S
				1	2	3
4	5	6	7	8	9	10
11	12	13	14	15	16	17
18	19	20	21	22	23	24
25	26	27	28	29	30	31

●:5 ☾:13 ○:20 ☽:27

PEOPLE IN HIGH OFFICE

Monarch - Queen Elizabeth II
Reign: 6th February 1952 - Present
Predecessor: King George VI
Heir Apparent: Charles, Prince of Wales

United Kingdom

Prime Minister
Edward Heath
Conservative Party
19th June 1970 - 4th March 1974

Canada

Prime Minister
Pierre Trudeau
20th April 1968 -
4th June 1979

Ireland

Taoiseach
Jack Lynch
10th November 1966 -
14th March 1973

United States

President
Richard Nixon
20th January 1969 -
9th August 1974

Australia	Prime Minister William McMahon (1971-1972) Gough Whitlam (1972-1975)
Brazil	President Emílio Garrastazú Médici (1969-1974)
China	Communist Party Leader Mao Zedong (1935-1976)
France	President Georges Pompidou (1969-1974)
India	Prime Minister Indira Gandhi (1966-1977)
Israel	Prime Minister Golda Meir (1969-1974)
Italy	Prime Minister Emilio Colombo (1970-1972) Giulio Andreotti (1972-1973)
Japan	Prime Minister Eisaku Satō (1964-1972) Kakuei Tanaka (1972-1974)

Mexico	President Luis Echeverría (1970-1976)
New Zealand	Prime Minister Sir Keith Holyoake (1960-1972) Jack Marshall (1972) Norman Kirk (1972-1974)
Pakistan	President Zulfikar Ali Bhutto (1971-1973)
South Africa	Prime Minister B. J. Vorster (1966-1978)
Soviet Union	Communist Party Leader Leonid Brezhnev (1964-1982)
Spain	Prime Minister Francisco Franco (1938-1973)
Turkey	Prime Minister Nihat Erim (1971-1972) Ferit Melen (1972-1973)
West Germany	Chancellor Willy Brandt (1969-1974)

JAN

4th | Rose Heilbron, one of the most outstanding defence barristers of the post-war period, becomes the first female judge to sit at the Old Bailey.

9th January: With a £5 million conversion into a floating university cruise ship nearing completion, the RMS Queen Elizabeth (renamed Seawise University) is destroyed by fire and capsizes in Victoria Harbour, Hong Kong. *Interesting facts: Launched on the 27th September 1938, Cunard's RMS Queen Elizabeth was the largest passenger liner ever built at that time and for 56 years thereafter. She weighed in at 83,637 tons, had a crew of over 1,000 and could carry 2,283 passengers. NB: She first entered service in February 1940 as a British troopship in the Second World War and it wasn't until October 1946 that she eventually served in her intended role as an ocean liner.*

9th | In a dispute over pay the National Union of Mineworkers hold a strike ballot and vote in favour of industrial action. The strike (the first official strike since 1926) lasts until the 19th February after which miners accept the governments offer of a 27% pay rise and a package of benefits worth £10 million.

18th | In a move that outrages militant Protestants, Northern Ireland Prime Minister Brian Faulkner bans all parades and marches in Northern Ireland until the end of the year.

20th | The number of people out of work and claiming benefit rises to 1,023,583, the first time it has risen above one million since the 1930s. *NB: It is almost double the 582,000 who were unemployed when Edward Heath's Conservative government came to power in June 1970.*

JAN

22nd	An anti-internment march organised by the Northern Ireland Civil Rights Association (NICRA) is held at Magilligan Internee Camp at Magilligan Strand, on the north coast of County Derry. The demonstration, made up of some several thousand protesters, is broken up by the army who use rubber bullets and CS gas to quell the protest.
27th	The British Army and the Irish Republican Army engage in gun battles near Forkhill, County Armagh; British troops fire over 1,000 rounds of ammunition.

30th January: Bloody Sunday: Thirteen unarmed civil rights demonstrators are shot dead and seventeen are wounded by British Army paratroopers in Londonderry, Northern Ireland. The protesters, all Northern Catholics, were marching in protest of the British policy of internment of suspected Irish nationalists. *NB: The killings brought worldwide attention to the crisis in Northern Ireland and sparked protests all across Ireland. Photo: The marchers at the top of Westland Street in the Bogside shortly before the shooting began.*

FEB

5th	In London 91 people are hurt and 122 arrested as mounted police charge a crowd of demonstrators protesting British policy in Northern Ireland.
9th	A state of emergency is declared by Prime Minister Edward Heath as a result of the month-long coal miners' strike.
22nd	The Official IRA bombs the headquarters of the British Army's 16th Parachute Brigade in Aldershot killing seven people. Claimed as a revenge attack for Bloody Sunday, the victims were all civilian staff and include Father Gerard Weston, a Roman Catholic British Army chaplain.
25th	Wings release their debut single "Give Ireland Back to the Irish" in the U.K. *Notes: The song is banned by the BBC, and Paul McCartney is condemned by the British media for his seemingly pro-IRA stance on Northern Ireland.*

Ford announces its new Granada model which is to be built at its Dagenham plant. Available as a saloon, coupé or estate car, it replaces the Zephyr / Zodiac and is designed to compete with the likes of the Rover P6 and the Vauxhall Victor.

3rd — Rock band Jethro Tull release their fifth studio album, Thick as a Brick. *Notes: The concept album, supposedly written by an 8-year-old Gerald Bostock, becomes a commercial success and is today regarded as a classic of progressive rock.*

4th — In Belfast the Abercorn Restaurant is bombed without warning killing two Catholic civilians and injuring over 130 people - the IRA does not claim responsibility for the bomb but are universally considered to have been involved.

4th — After over 100 years the last passenger train runs between Penrith to Keswick.

8th March: The GZ-20 Europa, the first Goodyear Blimp to be stationed outside the United States, takes to the skies for the first time at the Royal Aircraft Establishment in Cardington, Bedfordshire. *Fun facts: The Goodyear GZ-20 class blimp was first introduced in 1969 and remained the mainstay of Goodyear's airship fleet until 2017. Capable of carrying 6 passengers, the Europa was 58.67m long, had a gross weight of 5,824kg, and could travel at speeds of up to 50mph. Photo: The Europa moored outside the giant R101 sheds at RAF Cardington, 8th March 1972.*

9th — Four members of the Irish Republican Army die in a premature explosion at a house on Clonard Street in the Lower Falls area of Belfast.

13th — The United Kingdom and the People's Republic of China elevate diplomatic relations to the ambassadorial level.

17th	Ringo Starr releases "Back off Bugaloo" in U.K.; it peaks at No.2 and is his highest charting British single.
20th	The Provisional IRA detonate a car bomb in Lower Donegall Street, Belfast; four civilians, two RUC officers and a UDR soldier are killed while 148 people are wounded.
21st	Conservative Chancellor Anthony Barber announces a £1,200,000,000 tax reduction in the Budget. *NB: Barber's unsuccessful "dash for growth" leads to inflation, confrontation with the unions, and ultimately to the defeat of Edward Heath and his replacement by Margaret Thatcher.*
24th	The British government announce that the Stormont Parliament is to be prorogued and that 'Direct Rule' from Westminster will be imposed on Northern Ireland from the 30th March.
24th	William Whitelaw is appointed as the first Secretary of State for Northern Ireland.
25th	Vicky Leandros, singing "Apres toi", wins the 17th Eurovision Song Contest for Luxembourg at Usher Hall in Edinburgh.

26th March: After over 60 years of operation the U.K.'s last trolleybus system is closed In Bradford. *Fun facts: Since the demise of the Trolley Bus service in Bradford the system has flourished elsewhere. Today around 300 trolleybus systems are in operation in 43 countries around the world. Photo: Britain's last Trolley Bus, Bus No.844.*

31st	A crowd of more than 500 people attend a rally in London's Trafalgar Square to launch the latest leg of the Campaign for Nuclear Disarmament, a 56-mile Easter march from London to Aldermaston, Berkshire.
31st	The Official Beatles Fan Club, which has been run by the Beatles' secretary Freda Kelly since 1962, closes down.

11th	The radio comedy panel game "I'm Sorry I Haven't a Clue" is broadcast for the first time on BBC Radio 4. *NB: As of 2021 the show has aired over 500 episodes (excluding compilations and repeats) and is in its 74th series.*
18th	A report into the Bloody Sunday shootings by the Lord Chief Justice, Lord Widgery, exonerates British troops and blames the deaths on the march organisers for creating a dangerous situation where a confrontation was inevitable. His strongest criticism of the Army was that the "firing bordered on the reckless".

22nd April: Sylvia Cook and John Fairfax become the first two people to row across the Pacific Ocean, completing their epic 363-day journey from San Francisco to Hayman Island in Australia in a specially designed tandem row boat called Britannia II (designed by Uffa Fox). *NB: The achievement notably sees Cook become the first woman to have ever rowed across any ocean.*

20th	Francis Rowntree, an 11-year-old Catholic boy, is shot by a rubber bullet fired by the British Army in the Divis Flats area of west Belfast - he dies two days later. *NB: Rowntree's death is the first to result from the use of the rubber bullet.*
30th	The Brighton Belle train makes its final journey from London to Brighton. *Fun facts: The Brighton Belle was commissioned as the flagship of Southern Railway's mass electrification project, which commenced on the 1st January 1931. It was the world's only electric all-Pullman service and ran daily between London Victoria and Brighton.*

MAY

17th	Tottenham Hotspur complete a 3-2 aggregate win over Wolverhampton Wanderers at White Hart Lane to win the very first UEFA Cup.
18th	Queen Elizabeth II meets her uncle, Edward, Duke of Windsor (formerly King Edward VIII) for the last time at his home on the edge of Paris's Bois de Boulogne. *NB: The Duke of Windsor dies of complications from his throat cancer just 10 days later aged 77.*
18th	After receiving a bomb threat and a $350,000 ransom demand a Hercules aircraft from RAF Lyneham is scrambled to the luxury liner Queen Elizabeth 2. A crack four-man team including members of the SAS, SBS and RAOC bomb disposal parachute onto the liner only to eventually discover the whole affair is a hoax - they do find one suspect suitcase but after blowing the lock it contains nothing other than dirty washing. *Follow up: The "criminal mastermind" behind the crisis was 48-year-old shoe salesman Joseph Lindisi from New York - he was arrested, found guilty and sentenced to 20 years in prison.*
24th	Glasgow Rangers win the European Cup Winners' Cup, defeating FC Dynamo Moscow 3-2 in the final in Barcelona. *Notes: A pitch invasion by their supporters leads to the team being banned from defending the trophy the following season.*
26th	The travel firm Thomas Cook & Son is denationalised and is sold to a consortium of private businesses (headed by the Midland Bank) for £22.5m.
30th	The Official Irish Republican Army declares a ceasefire in Northern Ireland.
30th	The Angry Brigade, a far-left militant group who carried out bomb attacks in England between 1970 and 1972, go on trial at The Old Bailey. *Follow up: On the 6th December, in what becomes one of the longest trials in British legal history, four of the eight arrested receive 15-year sentences, reduced to 10 years after pleas of clemency from the jury; the other four are acquitted.*

JUN

5th	The funeral of The Duke of Windsor is held at Windsor Castle.
8th	South African born Tony Greig makes his Test Cricket debut for England against Australia at Old Trafford. *Fun facts: Greig played in 58 Tests and 22 One Day Internationals, and was captain of England from 1975 to 1977.*
11th	Former World Drivers' Champion Graham Hill and co-driver Henri Pescarolo of France win the 24 Hours of Le Mans with a healthy 11-lap margin over teammates François Cevert (France) and Howden Ganley (New Zealand).
16th	David Bowie releases his fifth studio album "The Rise and Fall of Ziggy Stardust and the Spiders from Mars". *Notes: The album would go on to receive widespread critical acclaim and make Bowie a household name.*
18th	British European Airways Flight 548 from London Heathrow to Brussels suffers a deep stall in the third minute of its flight and crashes killing all 118 passengers and crew; two passengers initially survive the accident but both die at the scene from their injuries. *NB: As of 2021 the crash remains the U.K.'s deadliest air disaster.*
23rd	Chancellor Anthony Barber announces he is to temporarily float the Pound.

JUL

1st	In London 2,000 participants take part in the first official U.K. Gay Pride Rally.

JUL

15th	Elton John's "Honky Chateau" makes it to the top spot on the U.S. Billboard album chart - hits include "Rocket Man" and "Honky Cat".
18th	Private James Jones becomes the 100th British soldier to die in the Northern Ireland Troubles. He is shot dead by a sniper whilst on sentry duty in Belfast.
21st	Bloody Friday: The IRA plant and explode 22 bombs in Belfast. In the space of 75 minutes 9 people are killed (six civilians, two British Army soldiers and one UDA volunteer) and approximately 130 others are seriously injured.
28th	Thousands of British dockers begin an official strike to safeguard jobs. *Follow up: The national strike continues for over a week after which the government proclaims a state of emergency (4th August). After several violent incidents and arrests, the Delegate Conference of the TGWU meet (17th August) and vote 53 to 30 to call off the strike and accept an amended Jones-Adlington Agreement.*
31st	Operation Motorman: Some 12,000 British troops, supported by tanks and bulldozers, smash through barricades and begin to regain control of the no-go areas established by Irish republican paramilitaries in Belfast, Derry and Newry. *NB: Operation Motorman is the biggest British military operation since the Suez crisis of 1956.*
31st	A few hours after the conclusion of Operation Motorman three car bombs explode on the Main Street of Claudy in County Londonderry. The attack, later referred to as Bloody Monday, kills nine civilians (five Catholics and four Protestants). No group claims responsibility but the IRA is suspected.

AUG

2nd	Gold hits record $70 an ounce in London (current record $2,061, 7th August 2020).
4th	Dictator Idi Amin orders the expulsion of 50,000 Asians with British passports from Uganda. Giving them 90 days to leave the country, Amin accuses them of "sabotaging Uganda's economy and encouraging corruption"
9th	The Tim Rice and Andrew Lloyd Webber musical Jesus Christ Superstar makes its West End debut at The Palace Theatre. *Fun facts: Running for over eight years, Jesus Christ Superstar held the record for longest-running West End musical before it was overtaken by Cats in 1989.*
10th	Paul and Linda McCartney are arrested for possession of six ounces of marijuana after a Wings concert in Gothenburg, Sweden. The couple are released after paying a combined fine of $1,200.
22nd	A bomb being planted by the IRA explodes prematurely at a customs office in Newry, County Down. The three IRA members kill six civilians and themselves in the explosion.
28th	The Queen's cousin, Prince William of Gloucester who is ninth-in-line to the throne, is killed in an air crash near Wolverhampton.

SEP

1st	The school leaving age in the U.K. is raised from 15-years-old to 16.
1st	The Second Cod War begins between the United Kingdom and Iceland after Iceland extends its fishing limits to 50 nmi (93 km).
11th	The television quiz show Mastermind is broadcast for the first time on BBC1.

13th September: French retail giant Carrefour opens the U.K.'s first hypermarket in Caerphilly, South Wales. At over 100,000 square feet the store is 10 times the size of anything that has preceded it and stocks every conceivable item from a thimble to a washing machine. *Photo: Christmas shoppers at Carrefour, Caerphilly, 1973.*

14th	The Ulster Volunteer Force (UVF) detonate a car bomb outside the Imperial Hotel near Antrim Road, Belfast, killing three people (including 91-year-old Martha Smilie, the oldest person killed during the Troubles) and injuring 50 others.
18th	One hundred and ninety-three Ugandan refugees, fleeing the persecution of the country's military dictatorship, arrive at Stansted airport in Essex. It is the first of hundreds of flights that will carry out the evacuation of Ugandan Asians to the United Kingdom.
19th	A parcel bomb delivered to the Israeli embassy in London kills diplomat Ami Shachori. *NB: The bomb was one of eight thought to have been sent by the Palestinian terrorist group Black September (the seven others were intercepted).*

OCT

5th	The United Reformed Church is founded out of the Presbyterian Church of England and the Congregational Church in England and Wales.
10th	Sir John Betjeman, Britain's most popular contemporary poet, is appointed Poet Laureate. *Note: Betjeman remained Poet Laureate until his death on the 19th May 1984.*
16th	The first episode of the soap opera Emmerdale Farm is broadcast on ITV. *NB: The title was shortened to Emmerdale on the 14th November 1989.*
16th	Rioting by inmates at the Maze prison in Northern Ireland causes a fire that destroys most of the camp.

17th October: Thousands of people turn out to welcome the Queen, Prince Philip and 22-year-old Princess Anne as they arrive in Belgrade, Yugoslavia. It is the start of a four-day state visit hosted by President Josip Broz Tito, and is the Queens' first state visit to a Communist country. *Photo: President Tito and his wife Jovanka with the Royal party shortly before attending a State Banquet at the Royal Palace in Belgrade.*

22nd	Gordon Banks, the England national football team goalkeeper, is involved in a car crash in his Ford Consul while driving on the wrong side of the road close to his home in Madeley Heath, Staffordshire. Fragments of glass perforate Banks' right eye and damage the retina. *NB: Banks' sight never returns leading him to retire from professional football the following summer.*
23rd	The Access credit card is launched by Lloyds, Midland and National Westminster banks. *Notes: Introduced to rival the already established Barclaycard, the Access card becomes defunct in 1996 when it is taken over by MasterCard.*
30th	The Northern Ireland Office issues a discussion document "The Future of Northern Ireland"; the paper states Britain's commitment to the union as long as the majority of people wish to remain part of the United Kingdom.

NOV

	The PEOPLE Party, a predecessor of the Green Party and the first political party in Europe to promote Green politics, is formed in Coventry.

6th	The Conservative Government of Edward Heath introduces price and pay freezes to counter inflation. *NB: Wages and prices had started to spiral out of control after the collapse of agreements between the previous Labour Government and the unions.*
11th	Great Britain win the Rugby League World Cup against Australia at the Stade de Gerland in Lyon, France.

18th November: In what is the first official women's international football game for both countries, England defeats Scotland 3-2 at Ravenscraig Stadium in Greenock. *Fun facts: Taking place almost 100 years to the day after the first men's international between the two countries, this historic match sees Sylvia Gore become the first woman to score for England and Mary Carr the first for Scotland. Photo: The England Women's football team in the changing room shortly before their game against Scotland.*

24th	Irish Taoiseach Jack Lynch meets with Prime Minister Edward Heath in London for a private dinner and talks about the situation in Ulster.
30th	Foreign Secretary Sir Alec Douglas-Home announces that Royal Navy ships will be stationed to protect British trawlers off the coast of Iceland.

DEC

10th	John Hicks is jointly awarded the Nobel Prize in Economics (with American Kenneth Arrow) for "pioneering contributions to general economic equilibrium theory and welfare theory".
10th	Rodney Robert Porter is jointly awarded the Nobel Prize in Physiology or Medicine (with American Gerald Edelman) for "discoveries concerning the chemical structure of antibodies".

WORLDWIDE NEWS & EVENTS

1. 1st January: Kurt Waldheim succeeds U Thant to become the 4th Secretary-General of the United Nations.

2. 1st January: International Book Year, proclaimed by the United Nations and made effective by UNESCO, begins.

3. 4th January: Hewlett-Packard introduces the $395 HP-35, the world's first scientific hand-held calculator.

4. 5th January: American President Richard Nixon signs a bill authorising $5.5 million in funding to develop a space shuttle. *Notes: The first space shuttle (Columbia) was launched from Cape Canaveral, Florida, on the 12th April 1981.*

5. 7th January: Iberia Airlines Flight 602 from Valencia, Spain, crashes into a mountain on the Balearic Island of Ibiza; all 98 passengers and 6 crew are killed in the crash.

6. 13th January: The Prime Minister of Ghana, Kofi Abrefa Busia, is overthrown in a military coup by Colonel Ignatius Kutu Acheampong.

7. 14th January: Margrethe II succeeds her father, King Frederick IX, to become the first Queen of Denmark since 1412 and the first Danish monarch not named Frederick or Christian since 1513.

8. 15th January: American world heavyweight boxing champion Joe Frazier stops Terry Daniels in 4 rounds to retain his WBC, WBA, and The Ring titles, at the Rivergate Auditorium in New Orleans.

9. 20th January: President Zulfikar Ali Bhutto announces that Pakistan is to begin the development of nuclear weapons.

10. 21st January: In India a New Delhi bootlegger sells wood alcohol to a wedding party which leads to the deaths of 100 people.

11. 24th January: Japanese WWII soldier Shoichi Yokoi is discovered in Guam after spending 28 years in the jungle.

12. 26th January: Yugoslavian air stewardess Vesna Vulović is the only survivor after her plane, JAT Flight 367 en route from Stockholm to Belgrade, explodes and crashes near the village of Srbská Kamenice in Czechoslovakia. She survives after falling 10,160 meters (33,330 feet) in the tail section of the aircraft; the 27 other passengers and crew are killed upon ground impact. *NB: Vulović holds the Guinness world record for surviving the highest fall without a parachute.*

13. 26th January: In Australia the Aboriginal Tent Embassy, a protest against the McMahon government's refusal to recognise Aboriginal land rights or native title in Australia, is set up on the lawn of Parliament House in Canberra.

14. 30th January: Pakistan withdraws from the Commonwealth of Nations after having been advised that Britain, Australia and New Zealand would recognise the Bengali Government in East Pakistan.

15. 31st January: King Birendra succeeds his father as King of Nepal.

16. 3rd - 13th February: The XI Olympic Winter Games are held in Sapporo, Japan. *Notes: It is the first time the Winter Olympic Games have taken place outside Europe and North America; Great Britain and Northern Ireland fail to win any medals.*

17. 6th February: The 29th Golden Globes award ceremony, honouring the best in film and television for 1971, are held in Los Angeles, California. The winners include the movie The French Connection, Gene Hackman and Jane Fonda.

18.	14th February: The Soviet unmanned spaceship Luna 20 is launched towards the Moon from the Baikonur Cosmodrome in Kazakhstan. *Follow up: Luna 20 successfully lands on the Moon on the 21st February and returns to Earth on the 26th February with 55 grams of soil from the lunar surface. Samples of the Luna 20 collection are shared with American and French scientists, and a 0.4983g sample is sent to Britain.*
19.	15th February: The President of Ecuador, José María Velasco Ibarra, is deposed for the fourth time in a coup d'état. Army commander General Guillermo Rodríguez Lara takes over as Acting President of Ecuador.

20. 17th February: The 15,007,034th Volkswagen Beetle comes off the assembly line in Wolfsburg, Germany, breaking a world car production record held for more than four decades by the Ford Motor Company's iconic Model T (1908-1927). *Fun facts: Production of the original Beetle continued until 2003 by which time 21,529,464 cars had been built - the final Type 1 VW Beetle rolled off the production line at Puebla, Mexico, on the 30th July 2003.*

21.	17th February: Italian tenor Luciano Pavarotti bursts into opera superstardom after an outstanding performance as Tonio in Donizetti's "La fille du régiment" at New York's Metropolitan Opera.
22.	18th February: Giulio Andreotti is sworn in as Prime Minister of Italy for the first time (he would later go on to serve two other terms as Prime Minister).
23.	21st February: President Nixon makes an unprecedented seven-day official visit to the People's Republic of China and meets with Mao Zedong. *NB: The visit marks the culmination of the Nixon administration's resumption of harmonious relations between the U.S. and mainland China after years of diplomatic isolation.*
24.	22nd February: Lufthansa Flight 649 is hijacked by five men armed with guns and explosives, and is taken to Aden. Passengers are released the following day after their $5 million ransom demand is paid in full by the West German government.

25. 1st March: John Lennon and Yoko Ono are served with deportation papers by the United States Immigration Service giving them fifteen days to leave the country. *Follow up: After a long battle against deportation Lennon eventually wins the right to stay in America on the 7th October 1975. Photo: Yoko Ono, John Lennon and their immigration attorney, Michael Wildes (right), leave the Immigration and Naturalization Service in New York City on the 16th March 1972.*

26. 1st March: Juan María Bordaberry is sworn in as President of Uruguay amid accusations of electoral fraud.

27. 2nd March: NASA's Pioneer 10 space probe is launched from Cape Canaveral, Florida. *Fun facts: The 258kg Pioneer 10 was the first spacecraft to traverse the asteroid belt, the first to complete a mission to Jupiter, and the first of five artificial objects to achieve the escape velocity needed to leave the Solar System.*

28. 14th March: Francis Ford Coppola film The Godfather, based on the book by Mario Puzo and starring Marlon Brando and Al Pacino, premieres at Loew's State Theatre in New York City. *Notes: At the 45th Academy Awards The Godfather is nominated for 10 Oscars, winning three including Best Picture and Best Actor for Brando.*

29. 14th March: Danish airliner Sterling Airways Flight 296 crashes into a mountain ridge on approach to Dubai, UAE; all 112 passengers and crew are killed.

30. 19th March: The Indo-Bangla Treaty of Friendship, Cooperation and Peace is signed forging close bilateral relations between India and the newly established state of Bangladesh.

31. 25th March: In Edinburgh Vicky Leandros wins the Eurovision Song Contest for Luxembourg with the song, Après Toi; The New Seekers come second for the United Kingdom with their song Beg, Steal or Borrow.

32. 27th March: The Russian space probe Venera 8 is launched to explore Venus. *Follow up: Venera 8 becomes the second robotic space probe to conduct a successful landing on the surface of the planet (22nd July 1972); Venera 7 was the first (15th December 1970).*

33.	10th April: The Biological Weapons Convention (BWC), a disarmament treaty that effectively bans biological and toxin weapons, opens with ceremonies in London, Moscow and Washington, D.C. *NB: The BWC entered into force on the 26th March 1975 after ratification by 22 countries including its three depositary governments (the Soviet Union, the United Kingdom, and the United States).*
34.	10th April: The 44th Annual Academy Awards, honouring the best in film for 1971, are held at Dorothy Chandler Pavilion in Los Angeles, California. William Friedkin's The French Connection wins five awards including Best Picture; the Best Actor and Actress awards go to Gene Hackman and Jane Fonda.
35.	10th April: An earthquake at Qir in Iran strikes with a magnitude of 6.7 on the moment magnitude scale and with a maximum Mercalli intensity of IX (Violent); 5,374 people are killed in the province of Fars.
36.	16th April: NASA's Apollo 16, crewed by Commander John Young, Lunar Module Pilot Charles Duke and Command Module Pilot Ken Mattingly, is launched from the Kennedy Space Center in Florida. The mission, focusing on science and the use of the Lunar Roving Vehicle (LRV-2), sees Young and Duke spend 71 hours on the lunar surface. Whilst there they carry out 3 moonwalks, drive more than 16 miles in the LRV, and collect 95.8kg of lunar samples. *Notes: Apollo 16 left lunar orbit on the 25th April and landed safely back on Earth on the 27th April.*
37.	23rd April: The 26th Tony Awards are held at The Broadway Theatre in New York City. The winners include the play Sticks and Bones, and the rock musical Two Gentlemen of Verona.
38.	25th April: Hans-Werner Grosse, a former German Luftwaffe bomber and glider pilot, glides a record 907.7 miles from his home city of Lübeck, West Germany, to Biarritz, France. *Fun facts: Set in a Schleicher ASW 12 over 11½ hours, Grosse's free distance gliding record stood for over 30 years.*
39.	1st May: The Pulitzer Prize for Fiction is awarded to Wallace Stegner for his novel Angle of Repose.
40.	5th May: In Italy an Alitalia DC-8 travelling from Rome to Palermo, Sicily, crashes with the loss of 115 lives. *NB: The crash is the deadliest single-aircraft disaster to occur in Italy.*
41.	9th May: Operation Linebacker, a large-scale bombing operation against North Vietnam by American and South Vietnamese tactical fighter aircraft, begins.
42.	13th May: A fire in a nightclub atop the Sennichi department store in Osaka, Japan, kills 118 people and injures another 78.
43.	14th May: The 14th Grammy Awards, recognising accomplishments by musicians in 1971, are held at Felt Forum in New York City; Carole King wins Record of the Year, Album of the Year, and Song of the Year; Carly Simon wins Best New Artist.
44.	15th May: The island of Okinawa reverts to Japanese control after 27 years of American rule.
45.	16th May: The world's first financial derivatives exchange, the International Monetary Market (IMM), opens on the Chicago Mercantile Exchange.
46.	18th May: In the United States basketball player John Sebastian makes a record 63 consecutive free throws while blindfolded at Maine East High School in Park Ridge, Illinois. *Fun fact: Sebastian's record lasts until the 5th February 1978 when it is beaten by the current record holder Fred L. Newman who makes 88.*
47.	19th May: "The Working Class Goes to Heaven" and "The Mattei Affair" are jointly awarded the Palme d'Or at the 25th Cannes Film Festival.
48.	21st May: In St. Peter's Basilica (Vatican City), Laszlo Toth attacks Michelangelo's Pietà statue with a geologist's hammer shouting "I am Jesus Christ - risen from the dead". With fifteen blows he removes Mary's arm at the elbow, knocks off a chunk of her nose and chips one of her eyelids.

49.	22nd May: The Dominion of Ceylon, under prime minister Sirimavo Bandaranaike, is proclaimed a republic and changes its name to the Republic of Sri Lanka. *Fun facts: Bandaranaike became the world's first female prime minister in 1960 when she was voted Prime Minister of the Dominion of Ceylon - she served three terms: 1960-1965, 1970-1977 and 1994-2000.*
50.	22nd May: The Magnavox Odyssey video game console is publicly unveiled at a press event at the Tavern on the Green in New York City. *Fun facts: The Odyssey (released September 1972) marks the dawn of the video game age and goes on to sell 69,000 units its first calendar year.*
51.	25th May: World heavyweight boxing champion Joe Frazier stops Ron Stander in 4 rounds at the Civic Auditorium in Omaha, Nebraska, to retain his WBC, WBA and The Ring titles.
52.	26th May: Richard Nixon and Leonid Brezhnev sign the Anti-Ballistic Missile Treaty in Moscow.
53.	30th May: Three Japanese Red Army members kill 26 people and injure 80 others in a terrorist attack at Lod Airport outside Tel Aviv, Israel. Two of the attackers are killed, while the third, Kōzō Okamoto, is captured after being wounded.
54.	31st May: In the 16th European Cup Final Ajax beats Internazionale 2-0 at De Kuip in Rotterdam (the two second-half goals are scored by forward Johan Cruyff).
55.	1st June: The musical drama film Cabaret, directed by Bob Fosse and starring Liza Minnelli and Michael York, is released in the U.K. *Fun fact: Cabaret holds the record for most Oscars earned by a film not honoured for Best Picture (8).*
56.	5th - 16th June: The United Nations Conference on the Human Environment is held in Stockholm, Sweden. It is the first world conference to make the environment a major issue and results in the creation of the United Nations Environment Programme (UNEP).
57.	6th June: An explosion at the world's largest coal mine kills 427 in Wankie, Rhodesia (now Zimbabwe). *NB: As of 2021 it remains the deadliest mine accident in the country's history.*
58.	14th June - 6th July: Hurricane Agnes strikes the east coast of the United States killing 128 people and causing an estimated $2.1 billion in damage ($13.72 billion in 2021); at the time it is the costliest hurricane ever to hit the United States.
59.	14th June: Japan Airlines Flight 471, a Douglas DC-8-53 from Bangkok, Thailand, crashes outside of New Delhi airport killing 82 of 87 occupants; 4 people on the ground are also killed.
60.	16th June: A rockfall inside a mile-long railway tunnel near Soissons, France, causes two passenger trains to collide and derail; 108 are killed.
61.	17th June: Watergate Scandal: Police apprehend five men (later determined to be White House operatives) at the Democratic National Committee headquarters at the Watergate Office Building in Washington, D.C. The five men, Virgilio Gonzalez, Bernard Barker, James McCord, Eugenio Martínez, and Frank Sturgis, are charged with attempted burglary and attempted interception of telephone and other communications.
62.	18th June: West Germany beats the Soviet Union 3-0 to win the UEFA European Football Championship (Euro 72) at Heysel Stadium in Brussels, Belgium.
63.	23rd June - 4th July: At the 22nd Berlin International Film Festival the Italian film "I racconti di Canterbury" (The Canterbury Tales), directed by Pier Paolo Pasolini, wins the Golden Bear.
64.	26th June: Nolan Bushnell and Ted Dabney co-found Atari, Inc. *Fun facts: Atari were responsible for the formation of the video arcade and modern video game industry. On the 29th November 1972, they released their seminal arcade version of Pong, the first commercially successful video game.*

| 65. | 28th June: In the United States President Nixon announces that no new draftees will be sent to Vietnam unless they volunteer for such duty. He also announces that a force of 10,000 troops will be withdrawn by the 1st September, which would leave a total of 39,000 in Vietnam, a major reduction from the 525,000 who were there when Nixon took office on the 20th January 1969. |

66. July: Actress Jane Fonda tours North Vietnam to speak out against the U.S. military's policy in Vietnam - whilst there she is photographed sitting on a North Vietnamese anti-aircraft gun being used to target American planes. *Follow up: The photograph earns her the nickname "Hanoi Jane" and effectively blacklists her in Hollywood.*

67.	2nd July: Following Pakistan's surrender to India in the Indo-Pakistani War of 1971, both nations sign the historic Simla Agreement with which they agree to settle their disputes bilaterally.
68.	8th July: President Nixon announces a three-year credit agreement to sell the Soviet Union $750-million of American wheat, corn and other grains. *NB: Described by administration officials as the biggest grain transaction in history between two nations, the U.S. government would go on to spend $300-million subsidising the purchase.*
69.	10th July: India's news agency reports that at least 24 people have been killed by stampeding elephants crazed by lack of water and food in the Chandka Forest.
70.	11th July: The long-anticipated chess match between world champion Boris Spassky of the Soviet Union and American champion Bobby Fischer begins in Reykjavík, Iceland. *Follow up: Fischer eventually defeats Spassky 12½ to 8½ on the 1st September.*
71.	21st July: A head-on collision between a holiday express and a local passenger train near Seville, Spain, kills 76 people.
72.	22nd July: Eddy Merckx of Belgium wins his 4th consecutive Tour de France.
73.	23rd July: NASA launches the first Earth-resources satellite, Landsat 1, from Vandenberg Air Force Base in California. *Fun fact: In 1976, Landsat 1 discovered a tiny 25m × 45m uninhabited island 12.4 miles off the eastern coast of Canada - the island was named Landsat Island after the satellite.*

74. 27th July: The McDonnell Douglas F-15 Eagle, a twin-engine all-weather tactical fighter aircraft, makes its first flight at Edwards Air Force Base in California. *Notes: The F-15 Eagle has been one the U.S. Air Force's primary fighter jet aircraft since its introduction in January 1976, with over 1,500 built (in all models) to date. Capable of a top speed in excess of Mach 2.5 (more than 1,600mph) the F-15 Eagle is among the most successful modern fighters with over 100 victories and no losses in aerial combat. Photo: Test pilot Irving L. Burrows prepares for the first flight of the pre-production YF-15A-1-MC Eagle at Edwards Air Force Base on the 27th July 1972.*

75.	1st August: The first article exposing the Watergate scandal (by Carl Bernstein and Bob Woodward) appears in The Washington Post.
76.	14th August: An East German Ilyushin airliner crashes shortly after take-off near East Berlin; all 156 on board perish in what is the deadliest aviation accident in Germany history.
76.	21st August: The satellite OAO-3 (Orbiting Astronomical Observatory) is launched from Cape Canaveral, Florida. *Notes: OAO-3 (named Copernicus after its launch) was a collaborative effort between NASA and the U.K.'s Science Research Council, and proved to be the most successful of the OAO missions. Copernicus operated until February 1981 and its success contributed to the instigation of the Hubble Space Telescope.*
77.	21st August: The oil super-tankers Oswego-Guardian and Texanita collide near Stilbaai, South Africa. The collision causes the Texanita to explode; it sinks within 4 minutes with the loss of 47 men.
78.	21st August: Scotsman Donald Cameron and Mark Yarry of New York City successfully complete the first crossing of the Swiss and Italian Alps by hot air balloon.
79.	22nd August: John Wojtowicz, 27, and Sal Naturile, 18, hold several Chase Manhattan Bank employees hostage for 14 hours in Brooklyn, New York (an event later dramatised in the 1975 film Dog Day Afternoon).

80.	22nd August: Trelew Massacre: At the Almirante Zar Aeronaval Base, Argentina, 16 detainees are executed by firing squad as revenge by the dictatorship for the successful escape of some of their comrades.
81.	26th August - 11th September: The 1972 Summer Olympics, officially known as the Games of the XX Olympiad, are held in Munich, West Germany.
82.	4th September: Swimmer Mark Spitz wins his 7th gold medal at the Summer Olympics in Munich, making him the most successful athlete at the games. *Fun fact: All seven of Spitz's gold medals were achieved in world record times.*
83.	5th - 6th September: Eleven Israeli athletes at the Olympics Games in Munich are murdered after eight members of the Arab terrorist group Black September invade the Olympic Village; five guerrillas and one policeman are also killed in a failed hostage rescue.
84.	10th September: Brazilian driver Emerson Fittipaldi wins the Italian Grand Prix at Monza to become the youngest ever Formula One World Champion at the age of 25.
85.	15th September: The five office burglars arrested on the 17th June at the Watergate Office Building in Washington, D.C are indicted by a grand jury for conspiracy, burglary, and violation of federal wiretapping laws. G. Gordon Liddy and E Howard Hunt Jr., who organised and directed the burglary, are also indicted. *Follow up: The burglars are tried by a jury officiated by Judge John Sirica and plead guilty, or are convicted, on the 30th January 1973. The Watergate Scandal: Witnesses later testify that President Nixon had approved plans to cover up administration involvement in the break-in. This, along with the administrations continual attempts to hide its involvement, became a major political scandal and eventually led to a constitutional crisis resulting in Nixon resigning from office on the 9th August 1974.*
86.	23rd September: Philippine president Ferdinand Marcos announces on national television the issuance of Proclamation No.1081 (signed 21st September) placing the entire country under martial law.
87.	25th September: A referendum in Norway sees 53.5% of Norwegians reject joining the European Economic Community.
88.	5th October: A speeding train crashes in Saltillo, Mexico, killing 208 people. *NB: The cause of the crash was attributed to the train's engineer and four crew members who had spent the day celebrating the upcoming Saint's Day drinking tequila.*
89.	13th October: Aeroflot Flight 217, a non-scheduled international passenger flight from Orly Airport in Paris, crashes on approach to Sheremetyevo International Airport in Moscow. All 174 passengers and crew are killed in what (at that time) is the world's deadliest aviation disaster. *NB: It was surpassed by the Kano air disaster in 1973 in which 176 people were killed.*
90.	13th October: Uruguayan Air Force Flight 571, a Fairchild FH-227D aircraft carrying 45 passengers and crew, crashes at around 14,000ft (4,300m) in the Andes Mountain range, near the Argentina / Chile border. *Follow up: Although 34 people initially survived the crash by the time they were rescued on the 23rd December, 72 days later, only 16 were left. They had suffered numerous hardships and had been forced to resort to cannibalism to survive.*
91.	15th October: The 61st Davis Cup concludes with the United States winning their fifth straight tennis title after defeating Romania 3-2 in the final in Bucharest.
92.	25th October: Tour de France winner Eddy Merckx sets a new world record covering 49.431km (30.715 miles) in an hour in Mexico City. *Fun fact: The record would stand for 12 years (until in January 1984) when Francesco Moser set a new record of 51.151km (31.784 miles).*

93.	26th October: Following a visit to South Vietnam, American National Security Advisor Henry Kissinger makes a surprise announcement at a White House press conference saying "We believe peace is at hand. We believe an agreement is within sight". *Notes: Kissinger later admitted that this statement was a major mistake as it inflated hopes for peace while enraging Nixon who saw it as weakness.*
94.	27th October: NASA loses contact with its Mars robotic space probe Mariner 9. *Fun facts: Mariner 9 reached Mars on November 14, 1971 and became the first spacecraft to orbit another planet. The probe greatly contributed to the exploration of Mars, mapping 85% of its surface and successfully returning 7,329 images over the course of its mission.*
95.	27th October: OPEC approves plan providing for 25% government ownership of all Western oil interests operating within Kuwait, Qatar, Abu Dhabi and Saudi Arabia.
96.	29th October: Lufthansa Flight 615 is hijacked by sympathisers of the Black September Organisation and threats are made to blow it up if the three surviving perpetrators of the Munich massacre are not released from prison in West Germany. The demands are accepted by the West German authorities leading to fierce condemnation by Israel.
97.	7th November: United Sates Presidential Election: Republican incumbent Richard Nixon defeats Democratic Senator George McGovern in a landslide winning 49 states. *Notes: With only 55 percent of the electorate voting, the election had the lowest voter turnout since 1948.*
98.	7th November: Attorney Joe Biden, representing the state of Delaware, is elected to the Senate after defeating long-time incumbent J.Caleb Boggs by 3,162 votes; Biden would win re-election to the Senate a further 6 times before becoming Vice President under Barrack Obama in 2009, and President in 2021.
99.	14th November: The Dow Jones Industrial Average closes above 1,000 (1,003.16) for the first time since its inception on the 7th October 1896.
100.	16th November: The United Nations Educational, Scientific and Cultural Organization adopts the Convention Concerning the Protection of the World Cultural and Natural Heritage.
101.	19th November: Seán Mac Stíofáin, the English-born chief of staff of the Provisional IRA, is arrested in Dublin after giving an interview to RTÉ. *Follow up: The interview is later used as evidence against him on a trial of IRA membership and, on the 25th November, he is sentenced to six months' imprisonment by the Special Criminal Court in Dublin.*
102.	19th November: West German federal election: Willy Brandt's Social Democratic Party becomes the largest party in the Bundestag for the first time since 1930, winning 230 of the 496 seats.
103.	30th November: A powerful explosion in a clandestine fireworks factory destroys an eight-floor apartment house in Rome, Italy; 15 people are killed an over 100 injured.
104.	2nd December: Australian federal election: The Labor Party led by Gough Whitlam defeats the Liberal / Country Coalition Government led by Prime Minister William McMahon. *Notes: Whitlam becomes the first Labor Prime Minister of Australia since the defeat of Ben Chifley in 1949. After being sworn in on the 5th December Whitlam's first action using executive power is to withdraw all Australian personnel from the Vietnam War.*
105.	3rd December: Spantax Flight 275, a Convair 990 Coronado charter flight from Tenerife to Munich carrying 148 passengers and 7 crew, crashes during take-off killing everyone on board. Many of the passengers are West German tourists heading home.

106. 7th December: NASA's Apollo 17, crewed by Commander Eugene Cernan, Lunar Module Pilot Harrison Schmitt, Command Module Pilot Ronald Evans, and five pocket mice (Fe, Fi, Fo, Fum, and Phooey), is launched from the Kennedy Space Center in Florida aboard a Saturn V rocket. The mission, focusing on science and the use of the Lunar Roving Vehicle (LRV-3), sees Cernan and Schmitt land in the Taurus-Littrow valley and spend more than 3 days on the lunar surface. Whilst there they carry out 3 moonwalks, drive more than 22 miles in the LRV and collect 243.7lb of lunar samples. *Notes: Apollo 17 left lunar orbit the 16th December and landed safely back on Earth on the 19th December - it is the last time that humans set foot on the Moon. Fun facts: The mission broke several crewed spaceflight records including the longest Moon landing, greatest distance from a spacecraft during an EVA of any type, largest lunar sample return, longest time in lunar orbit (6 days, 4 hours), and most lunar orbits (75). Photos: Apollo 17 on rocket launch pad LC-39A / The Apollo 17 crew: Harrison Schmitt, Eugene Cernan (seated) and Ronald Evans / Eugene Cernan on the lunar surface, 13th December 1972 / "The Blue Marble" image of Earth, taken on the way to the Moon from a distance of 18,000 miles, 7th December 1972.*

107. 7th December: Philippine First Lady Imelda Marcos is stabbed and wounded by an assailant with a foot long dagger - he is shot dead on the spot by her bodyguards.

108.	16th December: Operation Marosca: Portuguese commandos kill 300+ inhabitants of the village of Wiriyamu, in the district of Tete, Mozambique.
109.	18th December: As negotiations to end the Vietnam War collapse, Operation Linebacker II is launched with the aim of destroying major target complexes in the Hanoi and Haiphong areas. Over the next 12 days the United States Air Force carry out their largest heavy bomber strikes since the end of World War II.
110.	23rd December: A 6.3Mw earthquake strikes 17 miles northeast of Nicaragua's capital Managua. The quake causes widespread casualties among Managua's residents: 4,000-11,000 are killed, 20,000 are injured, and over 300,000 are left homeless.
111.	23rd December: On national radio Swedish Prime minister Olof Palme compares the American bombings of North Vietnam to atrocities committed under the Nazis; the speech leads to the expulsion of the Swedish ambassador from Washington.
112.	26th December: Ballon d'Or: Bayern Munich defender Franz Beckenbauer wins award for best European football player ahead of fellow Germans Gerd Müller and Günter Netzer.
113.	26th December: Former President Harry S. Truman dies in Kansas City, Missouri, at the age of 88.
114.	28th December: Kim Il-sung becomes president of North Korea.
115.	30th December: President Nixon orders a halt in the bombing of North Vietnam and announces that peace talks with the Hanoi government will resume in Paris in January.

BIRTHS

British Personalities

BORN IN 1972

Sarah Beeny
b. 9th January 1972

Broadcaster and entrepreneur.

Claudia Winkleman
b. 15th January 1972

Television presenter, film critic, radio personality and journalist.

Mark Owen
b. 27th January 1972

Singer and songwriter (Take That).

Steve McManaman
b. 11th February 1972

Footballer and television pundit who played 37 times for England (1994-2001).

Vicki Butler-Henderson

b. 16th February 1972

Racing driver and television presenter.

Darren Anderton

b. 3rd March 1972

Footballer who played 30 times for England (1994-2001).

Alex Kapranos

b. 20th March 1972

Musician, singer, songwriter, record producer and author (Franz Ferdinand).

Joe Calzaghe, CBE

b. 23rd March 1972

Undefeated World Champion boxer and International Boxing Hall of Fame inductee.

Nick Frost

b. 28th March 1972

Actor, comedian, screenwriter, producer, painter and author.

Priti Patel

b. 29th March 1972

Conservative politician who has served as Home Secretary since 2019.

James Cracknell, OBE
b. 5th May 1972

Athlete, rowing champion and double
Olympic gold medallist.

Richard Blackwood
b. 15th May 1972

Actor, presenter and rapper.

Archie Panjabi
b. 31st May 1972

Actress.

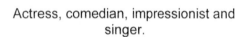

Debra Stephenson
b. 4th June 1972

Actress, comedian, impressionist and
singer.

James Martin
b. 30th June 1972

Chef and television presenter.

Peter Serafinowicz
b. 10th July 1972

Actor, comedian, director and screenwriter.

Jake Wood

b. 12th July 1972

Actor best known for his role as Max Branning in the soap opera EastEnders.

Geri Halliwell

b. 6th August 1972

Singer, songwriter, author, actress and philanthropist (Spice Girls).

Lawrence Dallaglio, OBE

b. 10th August 1972

World Cup winning rugby union captain who played 85 times for England.

Frankie Boyle

b. 16th August 1972

Comedian and writer.

Denise Lewis, OBE

b. 27th August 1972

Sports presenter and Olympic gold medallist in the Heptathalon.

Idris Elba, OBE

b. 6th September 1972

Actor, producer, director and musician.

Natasha Kaplinsky, OBE

b. 9th September 1972

Newsreader, television presenter and journalist.

Jimmy Carr

b. 15th September 1972

Stand-up comedian, television presenter, writer and actor.

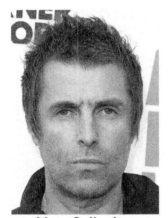

Liam Gallagher

b. 21st September 1972

Singer and songwriter (Oasis, Beady Eye).

Karl Pilkington

b. 23rd September 1972

Television presenter, author, comedian, radio producer, actor and voice actor.

Robert Webb

b. 29th September 1972

Comedian, presenter, actor and writer.

Matt Dawson

b. 31st October 1972

World Cup winning rugby union player who played 77 times for England.

Samantha Womack
b. 2nd November 1972

Actress, singer, model and director.

Thandiwe Newton, OBE
b. 6th November 1972

Actress.

Jonny Lee Miller
b. 15th November 1972

Actor.

Brian Molko
b. 10th December 1972

Belgian-born Scottish-American musician, songwriter and actor (Placebo).

Miranda Hart
b. 14th December 1972

Actress, comedian and writer.

Jude Law
b. 29th December 1972

Actor.

Notable British Deaths

15th Jan	Margaret Mary Julia Devlin (née Ashford; b. 3rd April 1881) - Writer known as Daisy Ashford who is most famous for her novella "The Young Visiters" which was written when she was just nine years old.
19th Feb	John Grierson, CBE (b. 26th April 1898) - Pioneering documentary maker often considered the father of British and Canadian documentary film.
20th Feb	Herbert Menges, OBE (b. 27th August 1902) - Conductor and composer.
25th Feb	Stephen Owen Davies (b. 1886) - Welsh miner, trade union official and Labour Party politician who was an MP from 1934 until his death.
29th Feb	Violet Trefusis (née Keppel; b. 6th June 1894) - Socialite and author.
21st Mar	David Fotheringham McCallum (b. 26th March 1897) - Concertmaster (principal first violinist) with the Royal Philharmonic Orchestra, the London Philharmonic Orchestra, and the Scottish National Orchestra.
29th Mar	Joseph Arthur Rank, 1st Baron Rank (b. 22nd December 1888) - Industrialist who was head and founder of the Rank Organisation.

25th April: George Henry Sanders (b. 3rd July 1906) - Actor whose heavy upper-class English accent and smooth bass voice often led him to be cast as sophisticated but villainous characters. With a career spanning over 40 years some of his best-known film roles include Jack Favell in Rebecca (1940), The Saran of Gaza in Samson and Delilah (1949), Addison DeWitt in All About Eve (1950) for which he won the Academy Award for Best Supporting Actor, Sir Brian De Bois-Guilbert in Ivanhoe (1952), and the voice of Shere Khan in The Jungle Book (1967). He also played Simon Templar, The Saint, in five films made in the 1930s and 1940s.

17th May	Sir Francis Gordon Lowe, 2nd Baronet (b. 21st June 1884) - Tennis player best remembered for winning the Australian Open in 1915.
22nd May	Cecil Day-Lewis, CBE (b. 27th April 1904) - Anglo-Irish poet who was Poet Laureate from 1968 until his death.
22nd May	Dame Margaret Taylor Rutherford, DBE (b. 11th May 1892) - Actress of stage, television and film who won an Academy Award for her role as the Duchess of Brighton in The V.I.P.s (1963).

28th May: Edward VIII (b. Edward Albert Christian George Andrew Patrick David; 23rd June 1894); King of the United Kingdom and the Dominions of the British Empire, and Emperor of India from the 20th January 1936 until his abdication on the 11th December of the same year. *Notes: Edward abdicated the throne to marry divorcee Wallis Simpson who was deemed politically and socially unacceptable as a prospective queen consort. After his abdication Edward was created Duke of Windsor. He married Wallis in France on the 3rd June 1937, after her second divorce became final.*

26th Aug	Sir Francis Charles Chichester, KBE (b. 17th September 1901) - Pioneering aviator, solo sailor and businessman. *Fun facts: Chichester became the first person to sail single-handed around the world by the clipper route and at the same time completed the fastest ever circumnavigation of the globe (27th August 1966 - 28th May 1967, a total of 226 days).*
28th Aug	Prince William of Gloucester (b. William Henry Andrew Frederick; 18th December 1941) - Grandson of King George V and paternal cousin of Elizabeth II. *NB: At the time of his birth he was the fourth in line to the throne (he was ninth in line at the time of his death).*
15th Sep	Geoffrey Francis Fisher, Baron Fisher of Lambeth, GCVO, PC (b. 5th May 1887) - Anglican priest and the 99th Archbishop of Canterbury (1945-1961).
28th Sep	Rory Storm (b. Alan Ernest Caldwell; 7th January 1938) - Musician and vocalist (Rory Storm and the Hurricanes).
1st Oct	Louis Seymour Bazett Leakey (b. 7th August 1903) - Kenyan-British paleoanthropologist and archaeologist.
2nd Oct	Sydney Charles Puddefoot (b. 17th October 1894) - Footballer who played for West Ham United, Falkirk and Blackburn Rovers. Puddefoot was also capped twice for England (1925-1926).
4th Oct	Colin Gordon (b. 27th April 1911) - Actor born in Ceylon who had a long career in British cinema and television from the 1940s to the 1970s.
15th Oct	Douglas Arthur Smith (b. 11th February 1924) - Radio announcer and comedian who spent 25 years with the BBC.
16th Oct	Leo Gratten Carroll (b. 25th October 1886) - Actor whose career lasted more than forty years.
5th Nov	John Reginald Owen (b. 5th August 1887) - Actor known for his many roles in British and American film along with television programs. *NB: Owen is perhaps best-known today for his performance as Ebenezer Scrooge in the 1938 film version of Charles Dickens' A Christmas Carol.*
10th Nov	Charles Hallows (b. 4th April 1895) - First-class cricketer who played for Lancashire and England. *Fun facts: In 1928, Hallows scored more than 1,000 runs in the month of May, a feat previously achieved only by W. G. Grace and Wally Hammond and never since. In his last innings of the month he still needed 232 runs to complete the 1,000 runs - he made 1,000 exactly and was dismissed with the very next ball!*
26th Nov	Richard Prescott Keigwin (b. 8th April 1883) - Academic who played first-class cricket for Cambridge University, the Marylebone Cricket Club, Essex County Cricket Club and Gloucestershire County Cricket Club, and played hockey for Essex and England.
28th Nov	Havergal Brian (b. William Brian; 29th January 1876) - Composer.
30th Nov	Sir Edward Montague Compton Mackenzie, OBE (b. 17th January 1883) - English-born Scottish writer, cultural commentator, raconteur and lifelong Scottish nationalist. He was one of the co-founders of the National Party of Scotland in 1928.
6th Dec	Janet Munro (b. Janet Neilson Horsburgh; 28th September 1934) - Actress who won a Golden Globe Award for her performance in the film Darby O'Gill and the Little People (1959) and received a BAFTA Film Award nomination for her performance in the film Life for Ruth (1962).
13th Dec	Leslie Poles Hartley, CBE (b. 30th December 1895) - Novelist and short story writer.
24th Dec	Gisela Marie Augusta Richter (b. 14th or 15th August 1882) - Classical archaeologist and art historian who was a prominent figure and an authority in her field.

1972 TOP 10 SINGLES

Royal Scots Dragoon Guards	No.1	Amazing Grace
Lieutenant Pigeon	No.2	Mouldy Old Dough
Donny Osmond	No.3	Puppy Love
Nilsson	No.4	Without You
The New Seekers	No.5	I'd Like To Teach The World To Sing
Chicory Tip	No.6	Son Of My Father
Gary Glitter	No.7	Rock And Roll (Parts 1 & 2)
T. Rex	No.8	Metal Guru
Neil Reid	No.9	Mother Of Mine
T. Rex	No.10	Telegram Sam

The Royal Scots Dragoon Guards
Amazing Grace

Label:	Written by:	Length:
RCA Camden	Judy Collins	2 mins 45 secs

The Pipes and Drums of the Royal Scots Dragoon Guards were first formed in 1946 and tour widely, performing in competitions, concerts and parades. Their most famous piece is "Amazing Grace" which reached No.1 in the charts in the United Kingdom, Ireland, Australia, New Zealand, Canada and South Africa, in 1972. The track sold over seven million copies and featured in the film the Invasion of the Body Snatchers (1978).

 Lieutenant Pigeon
Mouldy Old Dough

Label:	Written by:	Length:
Decca	Fletcher / Woodward	2 mins 44 secs

Lieutenant Pigeon are a novelty musical group who were popular in the early 1970s. Fronted by Rob Woodward and managed by him and drummer Nigel Fletcher, the other members included bassist Stephen Johnson and Woodward's mother, Hilda, who played piano. "Mouldy Old Dough" is the only British No.1 single to feature a mother and son.

Donny Osmond
Puppy Love

Label:	Written by:	Length:
MGM Records	Paul Anka	2 mins 58 secs

Donald Clark Osmond (b. 9th December 1957) is a singer, dancer, actor, television host and former teen idol. Osmond first gained fame performing with four of his elder brothers as the Osmonds, earning several top ten hits and gold albums. Then in the early 1970s he began a solo career, achieving several additional top ten records. Most recently Donny and sister Marie headlined an 11-year Las Vegas residency at the Flamingo Las Vegas (2008-2019). "Puppy Love" was Donny Osmond's first British No.1 record.

Nilsson
Without You

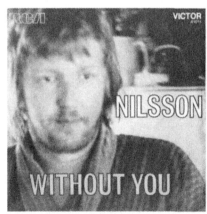

Label:	Written by:	Length:
RCA Victor	Pete Ham / Tom Evans	3 mins 16 secs

Harry Edward Nilsson III (b. 15th June 1941 - d. 15th January 1994), known professionally as Nilsson, was an American singer-songwriter who achieved the peak of his commercial success in the early 1970s. A tenor with a 3½ octave range, Nilsson's version of the power ballad "Without You" earned him the Grammy Award for Best Male Pop Vocal Performance in 1973.

5 **The New Seekers**
I'd Like To Teach The World To Sing

Label:	Written by:	Length:
Polydor	Backer / Davis / Cook / Greenaway	2 mins 23 secs

The New Seekers are a pop group formed in London in 1969 by Keith Potger after the break-up of his group, The Seekers. They achieved their breakthrough hit "Never Ending Song Of Love" in June 1971, and then went on to gain worldwide success with records such as "I'd Like To Teach The World To Sing", "You Won't Find Another Fool Like Me", and "Beg, Steal Or Borrow" (which placed 2nd for the U.K. in the 1972 Eurovision Song Contest).

---

6 **Chicory Tip**
Son Of My Father

Label:	Written by:	Length:
CBS	Moroder / Holm / Belotte	3 mins 20 secs

Chicory Tip are an English pop group formed in 1967. The group's greatest success came with their million selling song "Son of My Father", which is notable as the first U.K. No.1 single to prominently feature a synthesizer.

Gary Glitter
Rock And Roll (Parts 1 & 2)

Label:	Written by:	Length:
Bell Records	Glitter / Leander	Pt.1 - 3m 4s / Pt.2 - 3m

Paul Francis Gadd (b. 8th May 1944) is a former glam rock singer, known professionally as Gary Glitter, who achieved success in the 1970s and 1980s. Glitter sold over 20 million records and had 26 hit singles before becoming public hate figure after being convicted of downloading child pornography, indecent assault, child sexual abuse and attempted rape. The BBC no longer show any of his performances on repeats of Top of the Pops.

T. Rex
Metal Guru

Label:	Written by:	Length:
EMI	Marc Bolan	2 mins 24 secs

T. Rex were an English rock band formed in 1967 by singer-songwriter and guitarist Marc Bolan (b. Mark Feld; 30th September 1947 - d. 16th September 1977). The band was initially called Tyrannosaurus Rex and released four psychedelic folk albums under this name. In 1969 Bolan began to change the band's style towards electric rock and shortened their name to T. Rex the following year. T. Rex were pioneers of the glam rock movement and their recording of "Metal Guru" was the band's fourth (and final) No.1 single.

Neil Reid
Mother Of Mine

Label:	Written by:	Length:
Decca	Bill Parkinson	3 mins 59 secs

Neil Reid (b. 1959) is a Scottish former child singing star who won ITV's Opportunity Knocks in December 1971 singing his version of "Mother of Mine". When the song was released commercially by Decca Records shortly afterwards it went on to sell over 2.5 million copies globally. Reid's self-titled album also went to No.1 in 1972, making Reid the youngest person to reach No.1 on the U.K. Albums Chart at the age of 12 years 9 months.

T. Rex
Telegram Sam

Label:	Written by:	Length:
EMI	Marc Bolan	3 mins 45 secs

From 1970 to 1973, **T. Rex** encountered a popularity in the U.K. comparable to that of the Beatles, with a run of eleven singles in the top ten. They scored four British No.1 hits "Hot Love", "Get It On", "Telegram Sam" and "Metal Guru". The band's 1971 album Electric Warrior received critical acclaim as a pioneering glam rock album and also reached No.1 in the U.K. T. Rex were inducted into the Rock and Roll Hall of Fame in 2020.

1972: TOP FILMS

1. **The Godfather** - *Paramount*
2. **The Poseidon Adventure** - *20th Century Fox*
3. **What's Up, Doc?** - *Warner Bros.*
4. **Deliverance** - *Warner Bros.*
5. **Cabaret** - *Allied Artists*

OSCARS

Best Picture: The Godfather - *Produced by Albert S. Ruddy*
Most Nominations: Cabaret (10) / The Godfather (10)
Most Wins: Cabaret (8)

Best Actress Liza Minnelli and Best Supporting Actor Joel Grey.

Best Director: Bob Fosse - *Cabaret*

Best Actor: Marlon Brando - *The Godfather (declined)*
Best Actress: Liza Minnelli - *Cabaret*
Best Supporting Actor: Joel Grey - *Cabaret*
Best Supporting Actress: Eileen Heckart - *Butterflies Are Free*

The 45th Academy Awards, honouring the best in film for 1972, were presented on the 27th March 1973 at the Dorothy Chandler Pavilion in Los Angeles, California.

THE GODFATHER

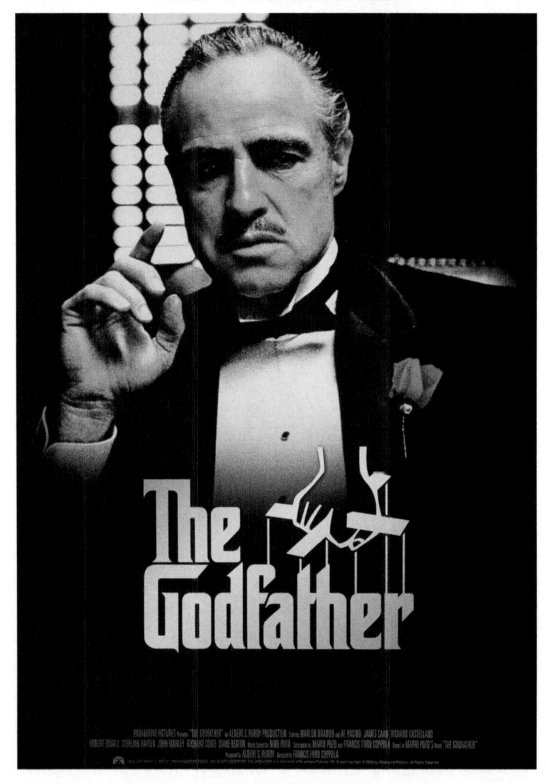

Directed by: Francis Ford Coppola - Runtime: 2h 55m

The Godfather follows Vito Corleone, head of the Corleone mafia family in New York, as he passes the mantel to his son Michael.

Starring

Marlon Brando
b. 3rd April 1924
d. 1st July 2004
Character:
"Don" Vito Corleone

Al Pacino
b. 25th April 1940
Character:
Michael Corleone

James Caan
b. 26th March 1940
Character:
Sonny Corleone

Trivia

Goofs	The use of the title Don in the film is incorrect as this term of respect is always attached to the individual's first name, not surname. Marlon Brando's character should have been addressed as Don Vito, not Don Corleone.
	When an old man sings "A Luna Mezzo 'O Mare" during the wedding celebration, his dentures can be seen coming loose. He re-sets his teeth without missing a note.
Interesting Facts	Marlon Brando wanted to make Don Corleone "look like a bulldog" so he stuffed his cheeks with cotton wool for the audition. For the actual filming he wore a mouthpiece made by a dentist.
	Francis Ford Coppola turned in an initial Director's Cut of the film lasting two hours and six minutes. Paramount Pictures production chief Robert Evans rejected this version and demanded a longer cut with more scenes about the family. The final version was nearly fifty minutes longer than his initial cut.
	The smack that Vito gives Johnny Fontane was not in the script. Marlon Brando improvised the smack and Al Martino's confused reaction was real. According to James Caan "Martino didn't know whether to laugh or cry".
	Al Pacino, James Caan and Diane Keaton were all paid just $35,000 for their work on the film.
Quote	**Michael:** My father is no different than any powerful man, any man with power, like a president or senator. **Kay Adams:** Do you know how naive you sound, Michael? Presidents and senators don't have men killed. **Michael:** Oh. Who's being naive, Kay?

Directed by: Ronald Neame - Runtime: 1h 57m

At midnight on New Year's Eve the SS Poseidon is struck by a 90-foot tidal wave and capsizes. The Reverend Frank Scott leads nine survivors as they try to escape the ship through steam, fire and rising water.

Starring

Gene Hackman
b. 30th January 1930

Character:
Reverend Frank Scott

Ernest Borgnine
b. 24th January 1917
d. 8th July 2012

Character:
Mike Rogo

Red Buttons
b. 5th February 1919
d. 13th July 2006

Character:
James Martin

Trivia

Goof | Linda Rogo had to change into her husband's shirt because she didn't wear a bra and couldn't climb in her gown. However, when she is in the smokestack about to climb the ladder a bra strap is visible. In the DVD commentary Stella Stevens acknowledged that she saw this error in the rushes and pleaded to have it removed, but to no avail.

Interesting Facts | Red Buttons and Carol Lynley, whose characters fall in love during the film, actually disliked each other intensely during filming. They refused to have anything to do with each other except when the cameras were rolling. Ironically, they ended up becoming great friends in later years.

While he and the others are lifting the giant Christmas tree, Rogo mutters, "Holy fuck, it's heavy". This was a genuine reaction from Ernest Borgnine and the line was kept.

Most of the exterior shots of the Poseidon were shot using a large miniature built from the original blueprints of the Queen Mary. The model is on display at the Los Angeles Maritime Museum at the Los Angeles harbour. The real Queen Mary is located just a few miles away in Long Beach.

Shelley Winters trained with an Olympic swim coach so that her character, who is a former award-winning swimmer, would come across more realistically in the underwater scenes.

Quote | **Captain Harrison:** *[over intercom to radio room]* Martin!
Martin, Wireless Operator: Yes, sir!
Captain Harrison: Get off a Mayday!
Martin, Wireless Operator: *[puzzled]* A Mayday, sir?
Captain Harrison: That's right, I said Mayday. Mayday, Mayday, Mayday!

WHAT'S UP, DOC?

Directed by: Peter Bogdanovich - Runtime: 1h 34m

The accidental mix-up of four identical plaid overnight bags leads to a series of increasingly wild and wacky situations.

Starring

Barbra Streisand
b. 24th April 1942

Character:
Judy Maxwell

Ryan O'Neal
b. 20th April 1942

Character:
Howard Bannister

Madeline Kahn
b. 29th September 1942
d. 3rd December 1999

Character:
Eunice Burns

Trivia

Goofs

When Mr. Jones is following Mr. Smith at the beginning of the film, Mr. Jones gets into a cab where the driver is very noticeably bald. When he gets out of the cab later the driver's hair has miraculously regrown and can been seen blowing in the breeze.

When the sign worker falls off the ladder the giant pane of glass breaks before his feet reach it.

Interesting Facts

What's Up, Doc? is the first American film to acknowledge stunt people in the credits - the first British film to do so was the James Bond film Moonraker (1979).

As his part was inspired by the stuffy professor played by Cary Grant in Bringing Up Baby (1938), Ryan O'Neal met with Grant. The only advice he received was to wear silk underpants.

What's Up, Doc? premiered at the 6,000 seat Radio City Music Hall Theater in New York City and during its first two weekends broke the house record that had stood since 1933.

Ryan O'Neal parodies one of his earlier performances. At the end of the film Judy Maxwell says "Love means never having to say you're sorry", a line from Love Story (1970), to which O'Neal's character, Howard Bannister, replies "That's the dumbest thing I ever heard".

Quote

Judy: You don't wanna marry someone who's gonna get all wrinkled, lined and flabby!
Howard: Everyone gets wrinkled, lined and flabby!
Judy: By next week?

DELIVERANCE

What did happen on the Cahulawassee River?

Deliverance

A JOHN BOORMAN FILM Starring
JON VOIGHT · BURT REYNOLDS in "DELIVERANCE"
Co-Starring NED BEATTY · RONNY COX · Screenplay by James Dickey Based on his novel
Produced and Directed by John Boorman · PANAVISION® · TECHNICOLOR®
From Warner Bros., A Warner Communications Company

Directed by: John Boorman - Runtime: 1h 49m

Intent on seeing the Cahulawassee River before it's dammed and turned into a lake, outdoor fanatic Lewis Medlock takes his friends on a canoeing trip they'll never forget into the dangerous American back-country.

Starring

Jon Voight
b. 29th December 1938

Character:
Ed Gentry

Burt Reynolds
b. 11th February 1936
d. 6th September 2018
Character:
Lewis Medlock

Ned Beatty
b. 6th July 1937
d. 13th June 2021
Character:
Bobby Trippe

Trivia

Goofs — As Ed is climbing down the rope from the cliff some shots show no tension on the rope even though he and the hunter's body are hanging from it.

When Lewis lays on the rocks after breaking his leg the flesh and bone sticking out of his leg changes between shots.

Interesting Facts — When John Boorman first tapped Jon Voight to appear in the film the actor was at a low point. His previous film, The All-American Boy (later released in 1973), was deemed an unsalvageable mess. Convinced his career was over, Voight credited Boorman with saving his life and then spending the next few months trying to kill him with extreme stunts during the filming of Deliverance.

Deliverance was Burt Reynolds' breakthrough role transforming him from a TV / B-movie actor into a film superstar.

While filming the white-water canoeing scene Ned Beatty was thrown overboard and was sucked under by a whirlpool. A production assistant dove in to save him but he didn't surface for thirty seconds. John Boorman asked Beatty "How did you feel?" and Beatty responded "I thought I was going to drown, and the first thought was, how will John finish the film without me? And my second thought was, I bet the bastard will find a way!".

To save costs and add to the realism local residents were cast in the roles of the hill people.

The film doesn't explain the title but the book states that what the city boys are trying to find in the backwoods is deliverance from the stress of modern life.

Quote — **Lewis:** Sometimes you have to lose yourself 'fore you can find anything.

CABARET

Directed by: Bob Fosse - Runtime: 2h 4m

In Weimar Republic era Berlin, Kit Kat club entertainer Sally Bowles romances two men while the Nazi Party rises to power around them.

Starring

Liza Minnelli
b. 12th March 1946

Character:
Sally Bowles

Michael York
b. 27th March 1942

Character:
Brian Roberts

Helmut Griem
b. 6th April 1932
d. 19th November 2004

Character:
Maximilian von Heune

Trivia

Goofs	When Brian thrusts the plate of cake at Sally the cake slides off the plate and slips down to her lap. In the next shot the cake is up on her chest. In "Money" Sally's nail polish is green at the beginning of the song, red in the middle, and green again at the end.
Interesting Facts	Cabaret won 8 Oscars, though not Best Picture. It lost that as well as Best Adapted Screenplay to The Godfather. As of 2021 Cabaret still holds the record for winning the most Oscars without winning Best Picture. English author Christopher Isherwood, who created the character of Sally Bowles for a 1937 short story, enjoyed the attention the film brought to his career but felt Liza Minnelli was too talented for the role. According to him Sally Bowles was based upon Jean Ross, a 19-year-old amateur singer who lived under the delusion that she had star quality, the antithesis of "Judy Garland's daughter". With this film Liza Minnelli was able to achieve something that her mother Judy Garland was never able to do, win an Academy Award. In fact the press speculated that Minnelli's Oscar was perhaps restitution for Judy being passed over for all those years.
Quotes	**Brian Roberts:** You're American. **Sally:** Oh God, how depressing! You're meant to think I'm an international woman of mystery. I'm working on it like mad. **Brian Roberts:** Aren't you ever gonna stop deluding yourself, hmm? Handling Max? Behaving like some ludicrous little underage femme fatale? You're... you're about as fatale as an after-dinner mint!

SPORTING WINNERS

BBC SPORTS PERSONALITY OF THE YEAR

Mary Peters (left) receives the BBC sports Personality of the Year award from Princess Anne (the previous year's winner) in London, 14th December 1972.

1972	BBC Sports Personality	Country	Sport
Winner	**Mary Peters**	**Northern Ireland**	**Athletics**
Runner Up	Gordon Banks	England	Football
Third Place	Richard Meade	Wales	Eventing

MARY PETERS - ATHLETICS

Lady **Mary Elizabeth Peters** LG, CH, DBE, DStJ (b. 6th July 1939) is a former athlete best known as a competitor in the pentathlon and shot put. At the 1972 Summer Olympics in Munich, Peters won the gold medal in the women's pentathlon, beating local favourite West Germany's Heide Rosendahl by 10 points to score a world record 4801 points.

Medal Record:

Championship	Location	Event	Medal
Commonwealth Games	Kingston, Jamacia (1966)	Shot Put	Silver
Commonwealth Games	Edinburgh, Scotland (1970)	Pentathlon	Gold
Commonwealth Games	Edinburgh, Scotland (1970)	Shot Put	Gold
Olympic Games	Munich, West Germany (1972)	Pentathlon	Gold
Commonwealth Games	Christchurch, New Zealand (1974)	Pentathlon	Gold

FIVE NATIONS RUGBY

Due the escalating political situation in Northern Ireland (and for fear that the troubles might spread to the Republic of Ireland) Scotland and Wales did not travel to Dublin to play their Five Nations matches. Therefore, although the remaining fixtures were fulfilled, no team could claim the title.

Table:

Position	Nation	Played	Won	Draw	Lost	For	Against	+/-	Points
1	Wales	3	3	0	0	67	21	+46	6
2	Ireland	2	2	0	0	30	21	+9	4
3	Scotland	3	2	0	1	55	53	+2	4
4	France	4	1	0	3	61	66	-5	2
5	England	4	0	0	4	36	88	-52	0

The 1972 and forty-third series of the rugby union Five Nations Championship saw eight matches played between the 15th January and the 25th March. Including the previous incarnations as the Home Nations and Five Nations, this was the seventy-eighth series of the northern hemisphere rugby union championship, and the first where a try was worth 4 points. *NB: The tournament saw France play its last matches at its decades-long home ground of Colombes, Paris.*

Date	Team	Score	Team	Location
15-01-1972	England	3-12	Wales	London
15-01-1972	Scotland	20-9	France	Edinburgh
29-01-1972	France	9-14	Ireland	Paris
05-02-1972	Wales	35-12	Scotland	Cardiff
12-02-1972	England	12-16	Ireland	London
26-02-1972	France	37-12	England	Paris
26-02-1972	Ireland	*Cancelled*	Scotland	Dublin
11-03-1972	Ireland	*Cancelled*	Wales	Dublin
18-03-1972	Scotland	23-9	England	Edinburgh
25-03-1971	Wales	20-6	France	Cardiff

CALCUTTA CUP

SCOTLAND 23-9 ENGLAND

The Calcutta Cup was first awarded in 1879 and is the rugby union trophy awarded to the winner of the match (currently played as part of the Six Nations Championship) between England and Scotland. The Cup was presented to the Rugby Football Union after the Calcutta Football Club in India disbanded in 1878; it is made from melted down silver rupees withdrawn from the club's funds.

Historical Records: England 71 wins / Scotland 41 wins / 16 draws

BRITISH GRAND PRIX

Emerson Fittipaldi on his way to winning the 1972 John Player British Grand Prix.

The 1972 British Grand Prix was held at Brands Hatch on the 15th July and was won by Lotus-Ford driver Emerson Fittipaldi over 76 laps of the 2.65-mile circuit; Ferrari driver Jacky Ickx was on pole.

Pos.	Country	Driver	Car
1	**Brazil**	**Emerson Fittipaldi**	**Lotus-Ford**
2	United Kingdom	Jackie Stewart	Tyrrell-Ford
3	United States	Peter Revson	McLaren-Ford

1972 GRAND PRIX SEASON

Date	Grand Prix	Circuit	Winning Driver	Constructor
23-01	Argentine	Buenos Aires	Jackie Stewart	Tyrrell-Ford
04-03	South African	Kyalami	Denny Hulme	McLaren-Ford
01-05	Spanish	Jarama	Emerson Fittipaldi	Lotus-Ford
14-05	Monaco	Monaco	Jean-Pierre Beltoise	BRM
04-06	Belgian	Nivelles-Baulers	Emerson Fittipaldi	Lotus-Ford
02-07	French	Charade	Jackie Stewart	Tyrrell-Ford
15-07	British	Brands Hatch	Emerson Fittipaldi	Lotus-Ford
30-07	German	Nürburgring	Jacky Ickx	Ferrari
13-08	Austrian	Österreichring	Emerson Fittipaldi	Lotus-Ford
10-09	Italian	Monza	Emerson Fittipaldi	Lotus-Ford
24-09	Canadian	Mosport Park	Jackie Stewart	Tyrrell-Ford
08-10	United States	Watkins Glen	Jackie Stewart	Tyrrell-Ford

The 1972 Formula One season was the twenty-sixth season of FIA Formula One motor racing. Emerson Fittipaldi won the championship for Brazil with 61 points from Jackie Stewart (United Kingdom, 45 points) and Denny Hulme (New Zealand, 39 points).

GRAND NATIONAL
WELL TO DO

The 1972 Grand National was the 126th renewal of this world famous horse race and took place at Aintree Racecourse near Liverpool on the 8th April. The winning horse was Well To Do who was owned and trained by Capt. Tim Forster. Of the 42 runners only 9 horses completed the course; 16 fell, 8 pulled up, 5 refused, 2 unseated their riders, 1 was brought down, and 1 was knocked over. *Photo: Race winner Well To Do at the Chair on the first circuit of the Grand National.*

	Horse	Jockey	Age	Weight	Odds
1st	**Well To Do**	**Graham Thorner**	**9**	**10st-1lb**	**14/1**
2nd	Gay Trip	Terry Biddlecombe	10	11st-9lb	12/1
3rd	Black Secret	Sean Barker	8	11st-2lb	14/1
4th	General Symons	Pat Kiely	9	10st-0lb	40/1

EPSOM DERBY - ROBERTO

The Derby Stakes is Britain's richest horse race and the most prestigious of the country's five Classics. First run in 1780 this Group 1 flat horse race is open to 3-year-old thoroughbred colts and fillies.

The 1972 Epsom Derby was won by Roberto and ridden by jockey Lester Piggott. In his short career (1971-1973) Roberto won seven of his fourteen races earning £339,902.

Photo (front right): American-bred, Irish-trained Thoroughbred Champion racehorse Roberto (1969-1988) going on to win the 1972 Epsom Derby.

FOOTBALL LEAGUE CHAMPIONS

England

Pos.	Team	W	D	L	F	A	Pts.
1	**Derby County**	**24**	**10**	**8**	**69**	**33**	**58**
2	Leeds United	24	9	9	73	31	57
3	Liverpool	24	9	9	64	30	57
4	Manchester City	23	11	8	77	45	57
5	Arsenal	22	8	12	58	40	52

Scotland

Pos.	Team	W	D	L	F	A	Pts.
1	**Celtic**	**28**	**4**	**2**	**96**	**28**	**60**
2	Aberdeen	21	8	5	80	26	50
3	Rangers	21	2	11	71	38	44
4	Hibernian	19	6	9	62	34	44
5	Dundee	14	13	7	59	38	41

FA CUP WINNERS - LEEDS UNITED

Leeds United 1-0 Arsenal

The 1972 FA Cup Final took place on the 6th May at Wembley Stadium in front of 100,000 fans. Leeds United won their first (and so far only) FA Cup 1-0 against holders Arsenal after fifty-third minute goal by Allan 'Sniffer' Clarke. *Photo: Leeds players celebrate their 1972 FA cup final victory; From left: Paul Reaney, Johnny Giles, Allan Clarke, Jack Charlton, Billy Bremner, Peter Lorimer, Norman Hunter and David Harvey.*

SNOOKER - ALEX HIGGINS

Alex Higgins 37-32 John Spencer

The 1972 World Snooker Championship was held between March 1971 and the 26th February 1972, with the final being held at Selly Park British Legion in Birmingham. Alex Higgins became the first qualifier to win the World Snooker Championship, defeating defending champion John Spencer 37-32 in the final and taking home £400 in prize money. Higgins also scored the highest break of the competition (133).

GOLF - OPEN CHAMPIONSHIP - LEE TREVINO

The 1972 Open Championship was the 101st to be played and was held between the 12th and 15th July at Muirfield Golf Links in Gullane, East Lothian, Scotland. Lee Trevino won his second straight Claret Jug (and the fourth of his six major titles) one stroke ahead of runner-up Jack Nicklaus (ending his bid for the Grand Slam). Trevino's winning share of the £50,000 prize fund was £5,500.

WIMBLEDON

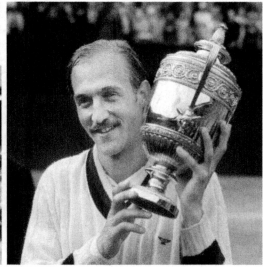

Men's Singles Champion - Stan Smith - United States
Ladies Singles Champion - Billie Jean King - United States

The 1972 Wimbledon Championships was the 86th staging of tournament and took place on the outdoor grass courts at the All England Lawn Tennis and Croquet Club in Wimbledon, London. It ran from the 26th June until the 9th July and was the third Grand Slam tennis event of 1972.

Men's Singles Final:

Country	Player	Set 1	Set 2	Set 3	Set 4	Set 5
United States	Stan Smith	4	6	6	4	7
Romania	Ilie Năstase	6	3	3	6	5

Women's Singles Final:

Country	Player	Set 1	Set 2
United States	Billie Jean King	6	6
Australia	Evonne Goolagong	3	3

Men's Doubles Final:

Country	Players	Set 1	Set 2	Set 3
South Africa	Bob Hewitt / Frew McMillan	6	6	9
United States	Stan Smith / Erik van Dillen	2	2	7

Women's Doubles Final:

Country	Players	Set 1	Set 2	Set 3
United States / Netherlands	Billie Jean King / Betty Stöve	6	4	6
France / Australia	Françoise Dürr / Judy Dalton	2	6	3

Mixed Doubles Final:

Country	Players	Set 1	Set 2
Romania / United States	Ilie Năstase / Rosie Casals	6	6
Australia	Kim Warwick / Evonne Goolagong	4	4

County Championship Cricket - Warwickshire

1972 saw the seventy-third officially organised running of the County Championship. It ran from the 3rd May to the 12th September and saw Warwickshire County Cricket Club claim their third overall title.

Pos.	Team	Played	Won	Lost	Drawn	Batting Bonus	Bowling Bonus	Points
1	**Warwickshire**	**20**	**9**	**0**	**11**	**68**	**69**	**227**
2	Kent	20	7	4	9	69	52	191
3	Gloucestershire	20	7	4	9	38	77	185
4	Northamptonshire	20	7	3	10	34	77	181
5	Essex	20	6	4	10	50	63	173

Test Series

England 2-2 Australia

1st Test: England won by 89 runs
2nd Test: Australia won by 8 wickets
3rd Test: Match drawn
4th Test: England won by 9 wickets
5th Test: Australia won by 5 wickets

Test	Ground / Date	Innings	Team	Score	Overs	Team	Score	Overs
1st	Old Trafford	1st	England	249	120.4	Australia	142	58
	08/06-13/06	2nd	England	234	86.2	Australia	252	85.2
2nd	Lord's	1st	England	272	91.5	Australia	308	122.1
	22/06 - 26/06	2nd	England	116	55.2	Australia	81/2	26.5
3rd	Trent Bridge	1st	Australia	315	118.4	England	189	88.3
	13/07-18/07	2nd	Australia	324/4d	92	England	290/4	148
4th	Headingley	1st	Australia	146	86.5	England	263	130.1
	27/07-29/07	2nd	Australia	136	56.1	England	21/1	10
5th	The Oval	1st	England	284	92.2	Australia	399	151.5
	10/08 - 16/08	2nd	England	356	121.2	Australia	242/5	92.2

One Day Internationals:

England 2-1 Australia

1st ODI: England won by 6 wickets
2nd ODI: Australia won by 5 wickets
3rd ODI: England won by 2 wickets

München  1972

The 1972 Summer Olympics, officially known as the Games of the XX Olympiad, were held in Munich, West Germany, from the 26th August to the 11th September. This was the second Summer Olympics to be held in Germany; the first had taken place in 1936 in Berlin under the Nazi regime. A total of 121 nations took part in the Games competing in 195 events over 21 different sports. Of the 7,134 athletes present 6,075 were men and 1,059 women.

British Gold Medallists:

	Competitor	Discipline	Event
1.	Mary Peters	Athletics	Women's Pentathlon
2.	Chris Finnegan	Equestrian	Three-Day Event Individual Competition
3.	Mary Gordon-Watson Richard Meade Bridget Parker Mark Phillips	Equestrian	Three-Day Event Team Competition
4.	Chris Davies Rodney Pattisson	Sailing	Men's Flying Dutchman

Medals Table - Top 5 Countries:

Rank	Nation	Gold	Silver	Bronze	Total
1	Soviet Union	50	27	22	99
2	United States	33	31	30	94
3	East Germany	20	23	23	66
4	West Germany	13	11	16	40
5	Japan	13	8	8	29
12	**Great Britain**	**4**	**5**	**9**	**18**

NB: The 1972 Summer Olympics were overshadowed by the Munich massacre which took place during the second week of the Games. Eleven Israeli athletes / coaches and a West German police officer at Olympic village were killed by Palestinian Black September members.

COST OF LIVING

FREE TRADE HALL, MANCHESTER

MEL BUSH in association with ASGARD

presents

Friday, 17th March

HAWKWIND

★ ★

STATUS QUO

SEATS 40p. 50p. 65p. 75p. plus booking fee

Advance Tkts. from—
HIME & ADDISON, (061) 834. 8019 & LEWIS'S

The Wilts Printing Works Ltd., Station Hill, Chippenham.

COMPARISON CHART

	1972	1972 (+ Inflation)	2021	% Change
3 Bedroom House	£8,460	£122,531	£235,243	+92.0%
Weekly Income	£17	£246.22	£621	+152.2%
Pint Of Beer	19p	£2.75	£3.94	+43.3%
Cheese (lb)	65p	£9.41	£3.04	-67.7%
Bacon (lb)	79p	£11.44	£3.20	-72.0%
The Beano	2p	29p	£2.75	+848.3%

FOOD & DRINK

Large Loaf Of Bread	10p
Anchor Butter (½lb)	14p
Stork Margarine (1lb)	11½p
Large White Eggs (dozen)	22p
Pint Of Milk	5p
McDougalls Self Raising Flour (3lb bag)	10½p
Mazola Pure Corn Oil	18p
Heinz Baked Beans	6p
Cadbury's Smash	10½p
Gale's Pure Country Honey (1lb)	19p
Heinz Mixed Fruit Sponge Pudding (10½oz tin)	9p
Ardmona Peaches (large tin)	14p
Maxwell House Instant Coffee (4oz jar)	25p
Coca Cola (can)	6½p
Digestive Biscuits	5p
Golden Wonder Crisps	3p
Johnnie Walker Whisky	£2.55
Haig Whisky	£2.55
Harvey's Bristol Cream	£1.25

CLOTHES

Women's Clothing

Tweed Raincoat	£7.45
Jacatex Blazer	£3.98
Simulated Ranch Mink Hood	£1.35
Lange's Nylon Tunic Top	£1.25
Honeystyles Courtelle Trouser Suit	£5.95
Super Quality Nylon Overalls	75p
Shirtwaister Crimplene Dress	£2.95
R. J. Wiltshire Button-Through Pinafore	£2.80
R. J. Wiltshire ¾ Lined Skirt	£1.40
Crimplene Polyester A Line Skirt	£1.25
Brentford's Quilted Dressing Gown	£1.99
Helga Satin Nightie	£2.50
Brentford's Quilted Yoke Negligee	£1.75
Oolala Seductive Underwear Outfit	£2.95
Estelle Teeny-Weeny Bra	£1.55
Simulated Nylon Knickers (x2)	£1.50
Winfield Panti-Hose	42p
Woolworth's Nylons	18p
Woolworth's Tights	15p
Anderson Spanish Suede Boots	£1.70
Simulated Leather Slippers	£2.15

Men's Clothing

Jacatex Winter Casual Coat	£4.98
Ex-Govt Reefer Coat	£3.25
Officers Raincoats (from U.S.A.)	£2.75
American Army Anorak	68p
Brentford's Smoking Jacket	£2.75
Freezebeaters Canadian Army Winter Cap	50p
Mr Harry Suit	£25-£40
Bib & Brace Overalls	85p
Western Warehouse Heavyweight Sweater	£1
Mr Harry Shirt	£4.40
Govt. Release Officers' White Shirt	65p
R. J. Wiltshire Stylish Crimplene Slacks	£2.50
Civil Defence Trousers	£1.25
Levi's Jeans	£1.25
Brentford's Nylon Pyjamas	£1.50
Leathercraft Shoes	£4.25
Winfield Socks	25p

The Uncrushable Mr Harry

Producing suits to your shape as well as your size is an exact science.

Mr. Harry goes even further.

He adds his unique flare for creating styles that get noticed without shouting.

(Mr. Harry, the great shirtmaker? The very same.)

Now something new has been added to the Mr. Harry Suit range; the uncrushable Harry Knit® Suits in Diolen.

These are not, Mr. Harry regrets obtainable everywhere. Not yet.

But keep asking. It's worth it to look so elegant and feel so comfortable. With no wrinkles whatever you get up to.

The Uncrushable Mr. Harry.

What you might call a sags to riches story.

Suit yourself from £25 to £40.

Mr Harry Suits
Designed to make you look slim.

Diolen
M

Illustrated, Mr. Harry Suit £29.50 and Mr. Harry Shirt £4.40

Silva-Thins 5/6 (27½p) for 20.

CHILDREN

Raleigh Chopper Bike	£35.60
Halfords Olympic Bike	£27.50
Smiley Pedal Car	£5.35
Woolworths Nurse Or Cowboy Outfit	£1.25
Skateboard	£3.62
Montrose 4-Ladder Climbing Tower	£10.97
Dawmet Paddling Pool	£4.99
Tracy's Tea Party	£6.28
Scalextric Set	£13.37
Monopoly	£1.35
Games Compendium	75p
Uno Card Game	£1.01
Table Tennis Set	75p
Dartboard Set	£1.09

ELECTRICAL ITEMS

22in Pye Colour TV (Currys)	£239
24in Ferguson B&W TV	£67
Sanyo 10in B&W TV	£56.75
PrinzSound System 8 Stereo Hi-Fi	£71.50
PrinzSound Stereo Amplifier	£32.95
Buccaneer Radio Tape Recorder	£26.75
Portable Communications & Radio Receiver	£8.99
Dixons Digital Clock Radio	£19.75
Zanussi Zoppas Refrigerator	£32.95
Servis Supertwin Washing Machine	£86.95
Indesit Europa Automatic Washing Machine	£78.75
Russell Hobbs K2 Kettle	£7.95
Kenwood Chef Mixer	£31.25
Plug-In Infa-Red Light Unit	£1.73
Concord Rotary Projector	£25.95
Prinz Cine Projector	£23.85
Sabre Super 8 Cine Camera	£19.50
Shopertunities Portable Electronic Organ	£7.97
Qualcast Concorde Electric Mower	£15.75
Black & Decker 2-Speed Power Drill	£7.60

YOUR MOTHER WOULDN'T LIKE IT.

1275cc. 94mph. 0-50 in 9·6 seconds*. £965. Handles well

From £965 incl. PT. Seat belts, delivery charge and number plates extra
Source: Autocar

MG The Great British Sports Car.

MG MIDGET

Mirror Shopping Clock up again by another 7p

A NOTHER massive leap in prices has sent the Mirror Shopping Clock zooming up 7p to £5·97½ this weekend.

Our shopping bill—an all-time record—was so steep that the Shopping Clock dial had to be re-drawn to show the rise.

Shock increases in the price of beef, lamb and coffee mean that our set basket of groceries now costs over 19 per cent more than it did when we began our survey eighteen months ago.

In the past four weeks alone prices have shot up by 5 per cent.

The main reason is sky-high meat prices—caused by lower supplies, panic-buying because of the threatened dock strike, and increased demand for our meat abroad.

Jumped

At my butcher's, best New Zealand lamb loin chops have jumped from 30p to 38p a pound in four weeks. They are 2p dearer than last weekend.

The price of a 2 lb. joint of topside beef has gone up this week by 2p to £1·20.

Apart from meat, we also had to pay 3½p more this weekend for a 4oz. jar of Maxwell House coffee.

Sainsburys, who have been selling it for some time at the splendid special-offer price of 22½p, have now raised the price to 26p.

At the branch of Tesco we visit I paid

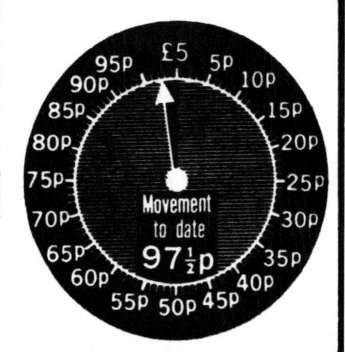

20p—½p less than last weekend (when I was overcharged) — for a packet of ten Birds Eye fish fingers.

So altogether our shopping bill came to £5·97½ compared with £5·90½ last weekend.

A ½p increase in the recommended price of Heinz 4½oz. beef dinner baby food, now priced 5½p, pushed our separate Toiletries List prices survey up to £5·12 this weekend.

Our third survey, the Men's List, remains at £5·68½.

The Grocer magazine this week reports another 117 grocery price increases, pushing the year's total so far to 3,510.

There were also twenty-three reductions.

Daily Mirror: Saturday 3rd June 1972

Miscellaneous Items

Ford Cortina	£1022
Mini 850	£695
Fiat 500	£599
Gallon Of Petrol	35p
Curry's 20in Ferguson TV Rental (monthly)	£3.20
Sussex 8ft x 6ft Garden Shed	£32.50
Silver Mist Greenhouse	£22
MFI Stainless Steel Sink Unit	£8.50
Solid Afro-Teak Monogram Fire Surround	£5.75
MFI Bunk Beds	£12.95
Starlight Luxury Headboard	£6.95
Brentford's Luxury Quilted Double Mattress	£12.95
Brentford's Quilted Nylon Bedspread (single)	£1.99
Brentford's Fitted Nylon Sheet (single)	£1.50
Mayman's Broadloom Carpet (sq. yd.)	60p
LS Warehouses Lounge Suite	£138
Cushionaire Inflatable Easy Chair	£2.95
Dixons 330 Zoom Telescope	£17.95
Prinz 8x50 Binoculars	£6.40
Praktica Super TL Camera	£55.95
Mastermatic III 35mm Camera	£12.25
Women's Synthetic Holiday Wig	£1
Cadets Cigarettes (20)	20½p
Woman's Own Magazine	6p
Daily Mirror Newspaper	3p
Daily Express Newspaper	3p
First Class Stamp	3p
Second Class Stamp	2½p

The other Viva saloon. 62·3 cubic feet of load space.

Engine: 1256cc and 1600cc. **Economy:** 35·2mpg.° **Top speed:** 82mph.° **Luggage space:** five feet of flat deck with the back seat down. **Comfort:** deep-sprung body-contoured seats, through-flow heating and ventilation, face-level adjustable fresh-air vents, 2-speed heater and demister. **Body:** steel up to 28% thicker than major rivals. Heat-sealed acrylic paint finish. **Rust-proofing:** price-included factory-applied underbody seal. Multi-stage phosphate anti-rust treatment. **Safety:** tandem master cylinder braking system, safety steering column, price-included front seat belts. **Prices:** Viva Estate 1256cc from £996, Viva Estate 1600cc from £1071.
° Daily Telegraph test. touring fuel consumption

Viva la Viva

VAUXHALL GM

"Does your window cleaner wear a bowler hat?"

"'Nightie-night' hell. I should have known better than to marry a scoutmaster!"

Laughter

"Family planning clinic — Boy! Have YOU got the wrong number!"

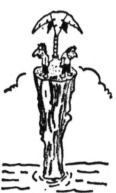

"I hate it when the tide goes out!"

"Say the word, Beryl, and it's four pints a day, a tub of cream, and all the yoghurt you can eat . . ."

Printed in Great Britain
by Amazon

86508800R00045